Little People, BIG DREAMS
ASTRID LINDGREN

Written by
Maria Isabel Sánchez Vegara

Illustrated by
Linzie Hunter

Frances Lincoln
Children's Books

Little Astrid lived with her parents and siblings on an old farm near Vimmerby, a small town in Sweden. Her childhood was very happy— so happy that she never wanted to grow up.

When she was four, her friend Edit read Astrid a story. In an instant, the room was filled with giants, witches, and fairies. They appeared from an object she hadn't really seen before: a book.

Astrid did her best to learn how to read. Once she started, she couldn't stop! For her, books were "almost unbearably wonderful." Before long, she had read her way through the library's collection.

One morning, she woke up with a terrible feeling.
Life suddenly seemed so complicated, and she didn't want
to play with toys as she always had. Astrid was growing up!

But being a young adult meant that she could be a rebel!
Astrid was the first girl in town to cut her hair short.
She then landed her first job at a newspaper. At age 19,
she become a single mom when her son, Lars, was born.

After a while, Astrid got married
and had a second child, named Karin.

Astrid was no ordinary mother! She loved playing, just like
a child, and was great at inventing stories.

One night, Karin got sick and asked her mother for
a get-well story about Pippi Longstocking: a funny
name she had just made up. "What a remarkable name!"
Astrid thought. "She must be a remarkable girl, too."

Pippi was more than remarkable...She was everything a child wanted to be! She lived alone with a monkey and a horse in Villekulla, her own cottage. She was free, happy, fearless—and the strongest girl in the world!

For many years, Astrid made up stories about Pippi for Karin and all her friends. For Karin's 10th birthday, Astrid put them down on paper as a present for her.

From beginning to end, Pippi's stories were delightful!
She was wise, honest, and wild. As soon
as the first book was published, she became
a heroine for readers all around the world.

Astrid wrote many novels and picture books about Pippi, which were translated into more than 100 languages. When Pippi made it to TV screens, Astrid worked on the screenplays, which become an important part of her work.

She created dozens of other memorable characters, like Rasmus, Ronja, Emil, and Lotta. Astrid received the highest recognition for her contribution to the world of books: two Hans Christian Andersen medals.

A Russian astronomer even named a planet in her honor: Planet 3204 Lindgren!

And still today, little Astrid—the girl who never wanted to grow up—lives in our heads and hearts when anyone reads Pippi Longstocking (who is always up for some fun!).

ASTRID LINDGREN

(Born 1907 • Died 2002)

1924

1971

Astrid Lindgren was born Astrid Anna Emilia Ericsson on a farm in
the town of Vimmerby in the south of Sweden. Spending afternoons
on hidden forest paths or roaming in fields of flowers, Astrid fell
in love with the world of nature and storytelling at an early age. In
the summertime, Astrid and her three siblings helped on the farm,
working in the fields and in the kitchens of the property. There, Astrid
discovered her first fairy tales, spoken over boiling pots of soup
and stew that she then recounted to her parents at bedtime. At age
thirteen, Astrid had her first story published in the *Vimmerby Times*,
and when she left school, she was hired by their editor in chief
to write copy for the newspaper. That year, Astrid had her first child,

1980   1987

Lars. She soon met her husband, Sture Lindgren, and a few years later, their daughter, Karin, was born. Both Karin and Lars grew up with their parents in a fun-filled apartment in Stockholm. When Karin asked her mother to make up a tale about a little girl named Pippi Longstocking, Astrid's free-spirited, unruly character came to life. The first book starring Pippi was published in 1945 and became a best seller, challenging stereotypes of what a young girl should be. One year later, Astrid became an editor at Swedish publisher Rabén & Sjögren, where she stayed for 30 years, writing Pippi's stories each morning before she went into work. Millions of copies later, the effervescent Pippi continues to delight readers young and old.

Want to find out more about **Astrid Lindgren?**

Read another great book:

Astrid Lindgren: Storyteller to the World (Women of Our Time)

by Johanna Hurwitz

BOARD BOOKS

COCO	MAYA	FRIDA	AMELIA	MARIE	ADA	ROSA	EMMELINE	AUDREY	ELLA

| 978-1-78603-245-4 | 978-1-78603-249-2 | 978-1-78603-247-8 | 978-1-78603-252-2 | 978-1-78603-253-9 | 978-1-78603-259-1 | 978-1-78603-263-8 | 978-1-78603-261-4 | 978-1-78603-255-3 | 978-1-78603-257-7 |

BOOKS & PAPER DOLLS

EMMELINE PANKHURST
ISBN: 978-1-78603-400-7

MARIE CURIE
ISBN: 978-1-78603-401-4

BOX SETS

WOMEN IN ART

WOMEN IN SCIENCE

ISBN: 978-1-78603-428-1

ISBN: 978-1-78603-429-8

Collect the
Little People, **BIG DREAMS** series:

FRIDA KAHLO	COCO CHANEL	MAYA ANGELOU	AMELIA EARHART	AGATHA CHRISTIE	MARIE CURIE

| ISBN: 978-1-84780-783-0 | ISBN: 978-1-84780-784-7 | ISBN: 978-1-84780-889-9 | ISBN: 978-1-84780-888-2 | ISBN: 978-1-84780-960-5 | ISBN: 978-1-84780-962-9 |

ROSA PARKS

ISBN: 978-1-78603-018-4

AUDREY HEPBURN
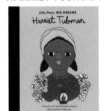
ISBN: 978-1-78603-053-5

EMMELINE PANKHURST

ISBN: 978-1-78603-020-7

ELLA FITZGERALD
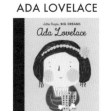
ISBN: 978-1-78603-087-0

ADA LOVELACE

ISBN: 978-1-78603-076-4

JANE AUSTEN
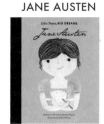
ISBN: 978-1-78603-120-4

GEORGIA O'KEEFFE

ISBN: 978-1-78603-122-8

HARRIET TUBMAN

ISBN: 978-1-78603-227-0

ANNE FRANK
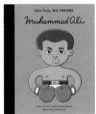
ISBN: 978-1-78603-229-4

MOTHER TERESA

ISBN: 978-1-78603-230-0

JOSEPHINE BAKER

ISBN: 978-1-78603-228-7

L. M. MONTGOMERY

ISBN: 978-1-78603-233-1

JANE GOODALL
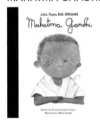
ISBN: 978-1-78603-231-7

SIMONE DE BEAUVOIR

ISBN: 978-1-78603-232-4

MUHAMMAD ALI

ISBN: 978-1-78603-331-4

STEPHEN HAWKING

ISBN: 978-1-78603-333-8

MARIA MONTESSORI

ISBN: 978-1-78603-755-8

VIVIENNE WESTWOOD

ISBN: 978-1-78603-757-2

MAHATMA GANDHI

ISBN: 978-1-78603-787-9

DAVID BOWIE
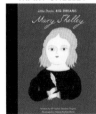
ISBN: 978-1-78603-332-1

WILMA RUDOLPH

ISBN: 978-1-78603-751-0

DOLLY PARTON

ISBN: 978-1-78603-760-2

BRUCE LEE

ISBN: 978-0-7112-4629-4

RUDOLF NUREYEV

ISBN: 978-1-78603-791-6

ZAHA HADID
ISBN: 978-0-7112-4641-6

MARY SHELLEY
ISBN: 978-0-7112-4639-3

MARTIN LUTHER KING JR.
ISBN: 978-0-7112-4567-9

DAVID ATTENBOROUGH
ISBN: 978-0-7112-4564-8

ASTRID LINDGREN
ISBN: 978-0-7112-5217-2

EVONNE GOOLAGONG
ISBN: 978-0-7112-4586-0

Brimming with creative inspiration, how-to projects, and useful information to enrich your everyday life, Quarto Knows is a favorite destination for those pursuing their interests and passions. Visit our site and dig deeper with our books into your area of interest: Quarto Creates, Quarto Cooks, Quarto Homes, Quarto Lives, Quarto Drives, Quarto Explores, Quarto Gifts, or Quarto Kids.

First Published in the USA in 2020 by Frances Lincoln Children's Books, an imprint of The Quarto Group.

400 First Avenue North, Suite 400, Minneapolis, MN 55401, USA.

T (612) 344-8100 F (612) 344-8692 **www.QuartoKnows.com**

First Published in Spain in 2020 under the title Pequeña & Grande Astrid Lindgren

by Alba Editorial, s.l.u., Baixada de Sant Miquel, 1, 08002 Barcelona

www.albaeditorial.es

A catalog record for this book is available from the British Library.

ISBN 978-0-7112-5217-2

Set in Futura BT.

Published by Katie Cotton • Designed by Karissa Santos

Edited by Rachel Williams and Katy Flint • Production by Caragh McAleenan

Manufactured in Guangdong, China CC122019

9 7 5 3 1 2 4 6 8

Photographic acknowledgments (pages 28–29, from left to right) 1. Astrid Lindgren, 1924 © Historic Collection / Alamy Stock Photo. 2. Lindgren, Astrid, surrounded by children, 1971© ullstein bild / Getty Images 3. Astrid Lindgren writer, 1980 © A.F. ARCHIVE / Alamy Stock Photo. 4. Astrid Lindgren Swedish author, 1987 © Roger Tillberg / Alamy Stock Photo.